COMPONENTS OF VOCAL BLEND

Plus "Expressive Tuning"

Gerald Eskelin, D.M.E.

Stage 3 Publishing
Woodland Hills, California

COMPONENTS OF VOCAL BLEND

By Gerald Eskelin, D.M.E

Published by: Stage 3 Publishing
5759 Wallis Lane
Woodland Hills CA 91367 U.S.A.

Manufactured in the United States of America

Library of Congress Control Number: 2004097966
ISBN 1-886209-30-8: $8.95 Softcover

Contents

ABOUT THE AUTHOR

The musical career of Gerald Eskelin is multi-faceted, spanning five decades of conducting, singing, composing, writing, and teaching. He has received two Grammy nominations for recordings with the L.A. Jazz Choir, which he founded in 1980. The group has performed and/or recorded with such notables as Rosemary Clooney, Steve Allen, and Al Jarreau.

The Gerald Eskelin Singers have been featured in a number of German television series, performing there with many well-known performers such as Glen Campbell, Frank Sinatra Jr., Herb Jefferies, and Tex Beneke. They have performed on various recording projects, most recently "Amazonia," a work by Bebu Silvetti, dedicated to the preservation of the rainforest. The singers have recorded hundreds of choral demos for a number of music publishers, including Hal Leonard, Shawnee Press and Warner Brothers.

Dr. Eskelin is equally at home in both classical and popular musical genres. His conducting experience includes almost everything from symphony orchestra to marching band and master chorale to pop choir. He has sung opera, show music, jazz, barbershop and even a bit of southern gospel.

Gerald Eskelin's academic credits include a Doctor of Music Education and Master of Arts degrees from Indiana University and a Bachelor of Arts degree from Florida Southern College. He recently retired from his position on the music faculty of Pierce College in Woodland Hills, California. Prior to his thirty-year tenure there, he taught at the University of Southern California and California Institute of the Arts.

ACKNOWLEDGMENTS

Over the decades, many choral artists have ignited my imagination and broadened my musical horizons. First among them is Fred Waring, whose weekly radio broadcasts during the 1940s would often bring tears of enjoyment to my young eyes. More recently, groups such as the Four Freshmen, the HiLo's, Manhattan Transfer and Take Six helped pave my personal pathway toward achieving my own measure of musical artistry. As a member of the American Choral Directors Association, I have attended a great many conventions where I heard the best of the best thrilling audiences with moving choral performances.

Also, I am deeply grateful to a great many gifted choral conductors in whose groups I was fortunate enough to sing during my formative years. I have particular fondness for Bruce Feighner, my a cappella choir teacher at Royal Oak High School in Michigan. Through my college years, I was able to observe an interesting mix of choral conductors, many of whom showed the way and some of whom were still searching for it. In both cases, I learned something valuable—what to do and what not to do.

I would love to be able to credit authors of books that systematically discussed the "secrets" of vocal blend. Unfortunately, I don't remember reading any. As a result, much of the credit for whatever wisdom is contained in these pages is due to the many hundreds of singers who have sung in my choral ensembles. They collectively provided an incredible workshop in which to hone the ideas and techniques described here.

The early drafts of this material go back to the mid-1980s, when it occurred to me that if I put down in writing some of the basic ideas I wanted my new singers to know, I wouldn't have to repeat them at the beginning of every semester, likely taxing the patience of my returning singers. As a result, I benefited from some of my more literate singer/readers who suggested better ways of expressing my points. Of particular help was Connie Marshall, who marked up my pages like a college English teacher.

My friend and colleague Scott Fredrickson, a talented and innovative college music teacher, also took considerable time in 1987 to evaluate the early draft. I have saved Connie's and Scott's suggestions in my "get to" files all these years and found them most valuable in shaping the final form of this writing.

Then, for more reasons than we have time to consider here, I put the draft aside until recently. Probably out of equal amounts of guilt and continuing enthusiasm for the project, I devoted most of 2004 to developing the book you are reading. I enlisted the help of a number of people to look over the later drafts and offer comments and suggestions. Some are people who have sung in my groups, some are people who have inquired as to when this book would be published, and some are people who are in neither category but whose opinion I hold in high regard.

Those readers who have sung with me and understand very well what I am trying to say include Linda Mays (Church of Our Saviour), Randy Ward (Air Force Academy Band) and Elin Carlson (Sixth Wave). When Peter Abood (Central Christian Church, Wichita KS), Jerry Pollard (musician) and Elizabeth Trice (graduate student) inquired about the availability of this book, it seemed like a good idea to ask them to check the draft for clarity. As it turns out, it was. My respected colleagues who agreed to look over the draft include Roger Duffer (Riverside College and Inland Master Chorale), Rollie Maxson (Arcadia High School), Mary Rago (Burroughs High School), Florence Riggs (voice teacher), Gene Townsell (church choral director and composer), Debbie Watkins (Weber State University, UT), and John Wilson (choral adjudicator).

The feedback I received from my readers proved most helpful in shaping the final text. I am grateful for their many suggestions for improvement and clarity as well as for their reinforcement of what they found helpful and informative. Finally, thanks to Stephanie Vitale for her editing, further improving my best efforts.

Gerald Eskelin

Prelude

As an adjudicator of high school and college choral festivals, I'm always thrilled to hear a student group that has it all—vibrant dynamic sound, elegant phrasing, and artistic musical expression. In such cases, it is evident that the director provided an environment in which the singers were able to develop excellent vocal techniques, impressive ensemble unity and expressive musicality. "Judging" such a group is largely a matter of complimenting the obvious.

On the other hand, I have heard many groups whose sheer enthusiasm for choral singing proves inadequate by itself to produce the performance level described above. Often, singers in such groups have had little or no exposure to fine choral singing. Given the meager offerings of quality choral music we find in the media, this is not surprising. And while local high school football games often appear on television, local high school choral concerts rarely do. In fact, choral music of any kind is virtually absent in the popular media except during the holiday season.

It would appear, then, that the primary responsibility for providing positive and gratifying choral experiences for singers with limited exposure rests with the choral music teacher. Playing recorded examples of fine singing is an obvious part of the solution, and is relatively easy to accomplish. More challenging, however, is teaching singers how to achieve the results they may have come to admire.

I have sometimes observed choral teachers focusing more on the imaginary music in their heads, than on the actual sound produced by their singers. They create a type of delusional "self defense" that blinds them to the actual condition of their choir.

Some teachers are in this predicament, ironically, because they themselves had excellent choral experiences. Quite likely, they were attracted to choral directing because of an inspiring music teacher. Large numbers of similarly enthusiastic future teachers flock to the best colleges to be further inspired by the finest choral directors academia has to offer. Since top-level collegiate choral ensembles normally consist of auditioned singers, there is often little need to "cover the basics." Spoiled by their own "Cadillac" choral experiences, they are often ill prepared for the shock when they encounter the "jalopy" sounds produced by their first high school choir.

Lacking skills to improve the sound of their choirs, many neophyte directors retreat into the hallucinatory state described above. They could easily escape this condition if they better understood the elements that lead to choral success.

When adjudicating choral groups, my primary responsibility is to provide encouragement and helpful suggestions. Whenever possible, I record my evaluation "live" so the director and singers can later review the audiotape and hear the performance characteristics that prompted each comment.

It has concerned me that such brief remarks on tape may not be thorough enough to be useful or fully understood by student singers, or even by many directors. This is largely why I decided to write this book. At the very least, it will help clarify my comments to the singers and directors whose performances I have adjudicated. At best, it will interest other choral directors and singers who wish to explore every possible means to a better performance.

As one might expect, most choral festival performances fall somewhere between perfect and embarrassing. Interestingly, I find myself making similar suggestions at nearly all of them. It occurred to me that my repetitiveness might simply be a result of a need to reiterate and reinforce my particular point of view; and, to some extent, this is probably true. On the other hand, since my scores have been generally in line with other judges, it may also be due to directors' general unawareness of certain factors that contribute to fine choral performance and how those factors can be successfully implemented.

Can vocal groups with assorted talent levels achieve a stunning blend? In my opinion, it is not differences in vocal training that prevent vocal blend, but rather an actual disregard for blend and/or the lack of awareness of the techniques necessary to achieve it. The primary purpose of this book, then, is to identify the elements that contribute to a beautiful choral sound and to provide methods and exercises by which to help actualize it.

The ideas and exercises herein are largely based on my own practical experiences working with singing groups—both amateur and professional. They are applicable to a wide variety of musical styles—from barbershop quartet to opera chorus—from the theater to the cathedral. Solo singers, as well, may find techniques here to enhance their artistry and professional cachet.

Most of the concepts in this book were originally contained in a "Read Me" supplied to singers who joined the L.A. Jazz Choir workshop, a training group that often led to a position in the professional group. Given that nearly all the members were experienced and accomplished singers, many with music degrees, their frequent remarks that these concepts were uniquely helpful to them seemed especially significant to me. It suggests that some of these views are not widely shared, in either the professional or academic world. In the event this is true, I am pleased to offer the ideas and practices that have proven helpful to my singers. I hope they prove helpful to yours, as well.

Gerald Eskelin

Components
of
Vocal Blend

CHAPTER ONE

Blend and Blendability

Opinions vary among vocal authorities in regard to matching vocal sounds. Some believe that in order to blend one must remove all or most of the natural characteristics from individual voices. Some believe that a choral group should blend when singing in certain styles—Renaissance, jazz or modern, for example—but need not blend when singing in other styles—including Baroque, Classical and Romantic. Others believe that when ensembles consist of sensitive and talented singers, blend will occur naturally, regardless of the musical style.

Some voice teachers and choral directors seem to fear even the notion of "vocal blend." Many directors are reluctant to "manipulate" singers' voices, and therefore tend to select singers who already have a voice appropriate to the sound they envision for their groups. Voice teachers who do not want their students exposed to "harmful practices" would likely support this approach. On the other hand, some teachers forbid their voice students to sing in a choir—any choir.

Singers themselves are sometimes quite unaware of the notion of vocal blend. More than a few singers, probably for a variety of reasons, accept the idea that their voice is their voice and they are more or less stuck with it. Some who have studied for years sing "the way I was taught" no matter what the ensemble environment. Some consider themselves to be "classical" singers, "pop" singers, "jazz" or "folk" singers.

On the other hand, there are singers who can blend with almost any vocal group, easily and quickly adjusting to the sound of a particular ensemble. Like chameleons, they virtually disappear into it. Such singers can enter a recording studio and become whatever the producer wants.

Are such flexible singers some kind of super breed, or can anyone do this? Is it advisable to aspire to become such a singer? Will singing in a variety of styles ultimately limit one's ability to excel in a single style? Answers to these questions are diverse, and I will not attempt to justify any of them. I will simply offer my opinion about vocal blending and you are welcome to any ideas here that you find practical.

I suspect that a significant part of anti-blend thinking arises from nebulous concepts of how vocal blend is achieved. I also believe that a reasonably intelligent singer can learn to perform well (and with healthy technique) in a wide variety of vocal styles and sound concepts. I have sung professionally in styles ranging from opera to bluegrass. To me, it is simply a matter of modifying "components" rather than changing basic vocal production. Healthy vocal sounds can be produced in many styles, just as unhealthy vocal sounds can be produced in any style.

What Vocal Blend is Not

Contrary to a popular belief, achieving vocal blend is not about eliminating individual vocal characteristics. Though it is generally easier to produce a blended choral sound while singing softly, it does not follow that a choir will necessarily sing less blended while singing loudly. On the contrary, component modification can promote blend in either circumstance.

Commonly, an ensemble singer exhibiting poor blending skills is asked to sing more quietly in order to minimize his or her offending sound. However, this does not really solve the problem. It simply results in a sound product that contains a quiet flaw. The hapless singer still injures the overall sound, particularly when all the other singers are producing a transparent blend.

Learning Vocal Concepts

Some singers appear to be "naturals" and exhibit an inherent knack for stylistic flexibility. Often with little or no formal training, they instinctively experiment with diverse vocal styles, sometimes developing remarkable sensitivity to sound varieties.

They can hear a particular sound characteristic and somehow automatically make appropriate vocal adjustments to simulate it.

Very likely, our own earliest attempts at human speech probably utilized this process. Once we heard the sound "ma-ma" enough times to conceptualize it, we discovered by experimenting that we could actually recreate that sound ourselves. We also learned that doing so earned the reward of parental delight. Thereafter, we developed language skills to whatever level satisfied our needs.

As we grew older, we settled into sound-skill habits that we came to regard as "my voice." We were told (directly or by inference) that we have a "great," "good," "fair" or "terrible" one. Believing this condition to be more or less set in stone, many singers tend to accept skills "appropriate" to their self concept. Some choral directors seem to buy into this misconception when they conclude that a certain singer "doesn't blend" and they simply leave it at that.

As suggested above, a common obstacle to achieving vocal flexibility occurs when a singer assumes that his or her teacher taught the "correct" way to sing. (Whether the student actually understood the teacher is another matter.) As a result, many ensemble singers are completely unaware that they might affect the sound adversely. When faced with this situation, choral directors often assume that careful diplomacy is the only means of relief.

A Better Way

However, diplomacy can be more effectively applied when the director is armed with helpful and effective suggestions for exploring change. In fact, *individual* diplomacy may not be needed at all when the suggestions are made to the group as a whole. Exercises in which singers are asked to imitate one another's voices—modeling both good and poor examples—is an excellent means of demonstrating that the human voice is a very flexible instrument.

Once singers experience the thrill of hearing the voices merge into a marvelous "oneness," new vocal self-images begin to emerge. The crusts that encased the old ones are shattered and, from that point on, the struggle is essentially over.

Once a singer abandons the "my voice" concept, development of vocal flexibility and sensitivity becomes possible. One needs only to reactivate the process of exploring and acquiring new sound concepts. When singers experiment systematically with the various components of vocal sound, their aural-to-vocal associative processes are reawakened. Whether or not a singer has a "good" voice, awareness of vocal sound components can make any singer a better blender—indeed, a better singer. And, if blending voices is a value shared by director and singers, the group thereby becomes a better ensemble.

It also becomes a more stylistically flexible ensemble. The group can readily modify its sound to accommodate a variety of choral traditions from opera to jazz and from the past to the present—indeed to the future. In my view, the key to this artistic kaleidoscope lies in understanding the vocal components that provide a rational and practical basis for achieving choral flexibility. Ultimately, it is this flexibility—guided by experience and taste—that opens a wide spectrum of possibilities in choral artistry.

CHAPTER TWO

Approach and Method

Voice teachers generally agree that asking a singer to directly engage specific muscles to modify vocal sounds can sometimes induce tension and, as a result, can reap constricted and unpleasant results. Of even more concern is that applying such practices can sometimes give a singer a false sense of "rightness." In the worst of cases, succeeding generations of teachers may continue to pass along these "right things to do" without really understanding what they were intended to accomplish.

I believe the safest and most effective way to train singers is to provide good vocal examples and to encourage students to emulate them. It is amazing how much can be accomplished simply by filling students' ears with good sounds. We all learned to speak by listening to others. There is every reason to believe that the same brain that figured out speech characteristics can learn to explore and imitate the sounds of good vocal production.

The Ears Have It

Fortunately, the ear can learn to hear and distinguish sound variations and to act as an automatic controller of the physical vocal apparatus. When this function is performed by the ear rather than by following verbal instructions, the voice responds with minimal conscious control of vocal muscles. The process can be expedited, of course, when a good teacher provides suggestions and reinforcement along the way.

Another premise on which this approach is based is that humans tend to think in terms of *concepts* attached to words and other symbols. This can be both a help and hindrance in assisting singers to develop vocal skills. Unfortunately, the terminology of vocal pedagogy often lacks consistency and precision. One teacher will use a term in one way while others use the same term to mean something else.

My intention here is not to settle questions of correct vocal terminology, rather, to remind us that a word is not equal to the concept it is intended to represent. The critical point here is that a student of vocal techniques be fully aware of the difference between words and perceptual information.

What's in a Word?

While words are very useful tools in general communication, they are quite inadequate in themselves to lead a singer toward improving his or her vocal skills. A vocalist who thinks he or she understands the *words* pertaining to vocal production may be in danger of stopping short of real insight into the *sounds* of vocal production. I fear that memorizing vocal terms and their definitions without having *experienced* their meanings does not lead to vocal success.

The word "cat" would make no sense to a child who has never seen one. That is why we have picture books to help youngsters build a practical vocabulary. But even a picture is not as helpful as experiencing a real cat. Similarly, a vocal term used to instruct a student who has not experienced its reference is equally meaningless. Yet some choral directors and teachers routinely ask their singers to "support," "focus the tone" or "sing in the mask" and assume they understand what to do.

To prevent a vocabulary of meaningless terms, words should be introduced only when the word's reference is being experienced. In effect, the new word helps to "point to" a sound characteristic *while it is evident.* In a sense, it really doesn't matter whether the term used is scientifically accurate or not. One could use "resonance," "placement," "ooga-booga," "george," or anything else, provided the student is focusing on the vocal component under consideration. On the other hand, it also wouldn't matter what word is used when the student *hasn't* focused on the experience.

Identifying Vocal Components

My purpose here is to help emerging vocalists to become familiar with the components, or variables, that are available to them, and to help them discover how they can modify vocal sounds by seemingly automatic physical adjustments directed by the ear. Once these skills are learned, there is little need for words anyway, since the singer will make intuitive adjustments according to what the ear reports to the brain.

Of course, a vocabulary of terms will be very practical when a director wants his or her singers to modify a particular sound component that was previously identified. Sometimes the request will be a reminder to singers who have wandered from the consensus. At other times the request might be addressed to the group as a whole toward modifying a certain component for the sake of artistic or stylistic considerations. In such cases, words can be effective tools of communication provided all of the singers are aware of both their meaning and their application to the sound.

My intention here is to describe my own experience with these components (as I have defined them) and to show how one can use these ideas to develop vocal sound awareness in singers. I am not particularly concerned here with systematic or scientific verification, although that might be an interesting pursuit. I am only reporting here what has worked for me. And why shouldn't it work? It simply relies on the basic and natural function of acquiring vocal sound skills through the use of that marvelous piece of machinery—the human ear.

In this book, I have named the various components using terms that seemed practical to me. As you may now realize, I would have no problem if you elected to use different terms with your singers when you feel a better term is applicable. In fact, you might consider a completely different organization of perceptual components if you feel mine are not practical for you.

The important thing is to offer singers an opportunity to become more aware of the variety of sounds available to them and how to use that variety for enhancing artistic expression. Naturally, the direction of exploration and the artistic result will vary according to the stylistic preferences of the singers and director. That is as it should be. Nevertheless, the process is the same—letting the ear perform its essential function of discriminating between sounds that contribute to a specific blend and those that tend to injure it.

CHAPTER THREE
Vocal Concepts and Vocabulary

Words are surely the most helpful tools we have for conducting and organizing our daily lives. We commonly use words taking little thought for their literal and separate meanings, and easily combine them into complex expressions. "I'll be a little late, so go ahead and start without me," incorporates nearly a dozen separate concepts, and successful communication requires that the users —both speaker and listener—share similar meanings for these phrases.

However, words can actually obscure communication when users haven't connected them to similar concepts. For example, when a music appreciation student was asked to describe a recorded passage heard in class, he said, "The music went up." Given my own sense of the word "up" used in a musical context, I naturally assumed he was referring to pitch. Since the passage actually did not rise in pitch, I had the options of assuming that he had poor pitch perception or that he was using the word "up" to represent a different sound concept.

With a bit of probing, I discovered the problem consisted mostly of the latter but not totally excluding the former. The student had referred to increased loudness (an accurate observation) as "up," but also had not yet focused on "loudness" *and* "pitch" as independent perceptual concepts. Evidently, the musical passage was experienced as "having some sort of increasing intensity."

Since that experience, I have discovered that many people suffer from this same verbal/conceptual confusion. Because they have not isolated and "conceived" these two very different perceptual experiences, they lack the ability to refer to them using meaningful vocabulary. No amount of verbal lecturing or careful defining can rescue the sufferer from this condition. Dissertations on decibels or cycles per second will not do it. Only by experiencing and focusing on each *perception*—separately—can a student discover the difference.

We teachers can and should borrow a very helpful tool from researchers called "the scientific method." In order to gain information about what goes on inside a complex process, the researcher isolates individual variables by holding constant all qualities but one, and observing changes in that one when affected by changing circumstances. Once isolated, a variable can be named and treated as a separate concept even though it cannot physically exist apart from the experience as a whole.

Using this technique, teaching perceptual concepts consists of providing experiences in which irrelevant data is held constant while varying only the feature to be learned. The student's attention can then focus on the "moving" attribute. It's simply a matter of continuity and contrast—the basis of all human knowledge. Once the student vividly experiences a given feature, the teacher needs only to name it. Thereafter, that vocabulary is properly attached to that specific attribute.

This teaching technique is vital in helping singers gain insight regarding the factors that affect vocal sounds. For example, in order to isolate the vocal quality "brightness," all other factors such as "pitch," "vowel," "resonance," and "density" must be held constant. While experimenting with various muscle movements —directed by the ear—one learns *which* movements seem to affect "brightness" and how they affect it.

Exploring the range of "brightness" facilitates a singer's use of that variable to modify the sound. Similar experimentation and practice with other variables increases the ability to use more and more factors, some of which remain unnamed. Eventually, the vocal artist applies modifications automatically and without conscious effort. The soloist has increased the number of tools available to modify vocal sounds for expressive effect. The ensemble singer, through careful listening, has increased experience in matching sounds with other sensitive singers.

Components and Terminology

While this may sound simple in theory, there are at least two factors that make learning "vocal components" somewhat problematic. One of these is that the variables are not physically independent of one another. Some vowel sounds are naturally brighter than others, therefore, a singer must learn to adjust brightness appropriately as the vowel changes in order to maintain a uniform brightness in the phrase. This inter-relationship of vocal sound components frequently results in difficulty in isolating them. A novice singer will often change brightness when asked to adjust vowel. In order to break through this obstacle, one needs to be diligent while conceptualizing the two separate variables and learn to recognize their unique quality.

Another factor that impedes learning vocal components is that the terminology of vocal practice is often a tangled web of miscommunication. What some people call "vowel focus", others call "resonance," "placement" or something else. I suspect that when voice teachers warn students about considering another voice teacher's "method," the differences may be only a matter of terminology.

There actually may be more agreement in practice than this apparent disagreement of terminology would suggest. Or perhaps talented students are intuitive enough to succeed in spite of terminology. In either case, it is important to remember that the object of this book is not to standardize vocal terms. Rather, it is to describe a technique by which singers can get in touch with the components of vocal sound, regardless of specific terminology, and thereby achieve results they can hear for themselves.

For our purposes, I will use the terms "vowel," "brightness," "resonance," "nasality," "pitch," "density," "loudness," and "phrasing" to represent what I see as the basic components of vocal blend. Some of these topics will require considerable pages in order to share the suggestions I have to make. Others will require very few pages.

You may have noticed that I did not include a chapter on "vibrato," a rather common consideration in regard to vocal blend. The reason is that I have little or no suggestions on that topic; although I believe vibrato can be modified by the same process as other components, namely, experimenting with physical adjustments guided by the ear.

CHAPTER FOUR

Vowel

If there is one component more important to vocal blend than all the others, it is surely vowel. While good intonation is vital to good blend, pitch agreement is very difficult to achieve when singers disagree on vowel focus. Once vowel is in agreement, intonation improves with little effort. Therefore, understanding vowel would seem the best way to begin exploring the components.

You may have noticed that the title of this chapter is "Vowel"—not "Vowels." That choice was made for a very important reason. The traditional concept of "five vowels" ("ay-ee," "ee," "ah-ee," "oh-oo" and "ee-oo") has caused countless "trained" singers to become encrusted in vocal habits that limit flexibility and sensitivity to the full spectrum of vowel possibilities. Just as "loudness," "pitch," and other components can be modified *gradually*, so can vowel be adjusted in a seamless continuum.

The use of the symbols *pp, p, mp, mf, f* and *ff* do not cause singers to leap from one degree of loudness to another as if they were absolute values. Singers generally flow through musical dynamics with flexibility and sensitivity, using the symbols as approximations and letting the ear indicate the specific loudness needed to achieve an artistic performance. But when focusing vowel, many singers ignore what they hear from their fellow singers and simply make sounds they assume are correct. The result is all too frequently a battle of conflicting sounds.

Vowel as Timbre

From a vocal standpoint, "vowel" is simply another name for "timbre." We are able to recognize the sounds of musical instruments by differences in their acoustic timbral patterns. These differences are caused by changes in relative strengths of acoustic partials—sometimes called overtones. A similar phenomenon takes place when vowel is changed vocally. The sound of a pure "ee" is very different from the sound of a pure "oo." In a sense, they are simply "different instruments" created by changing the relative strengths of partials.

Watching patterns of partials change on an oscilloscope is not required for learning vowel focus. Although that would undoubtedly be interesting and informative, simple listening can do the job very well when combined with vocal exploration. In short, one must *participate* in the process. By experimenting with vowel sounds, one can discover the physical movements that cause vocal tone to modify the timbre toward a particular vowel focus.

The chart below represents a spatial relationship of vowel sounds. It is not unlike other such charts in that it reflects the spectrum of common vowel sounds found in acoustical analysis of speech. It places the sounds in terms of front/back and high/low relationships. These relative locations transfer easily and logically to physical vocal adjustments, helping singers to visualize the spatial relationships as they explore the sound relationships.

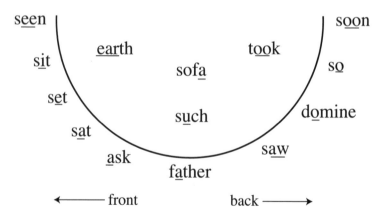

The words on this chart are to be considered reference points along a continuum, not as "correct" placements. Each reference word locates a point of vowel sound relative to other points. Since spoken language uses a great number of subtle vowel adjustments, the number of reference words used on the chart is quite arbitrary.

Many more "standard" words could be added but this might tend to clutter rather than clarify.

For example, standard phonetic alphabets use the same symbol for the vowel sounds in the words "sit" and "sing." Yet, the commonly used vowel location for the word "sing" is slightly higher than for the word "sit." Try this experiment to see whether this is your preference. Say the word "sit" and repeat the vowel sound a few times to let it register in your memory. Then use that same vowel sound while saying the word "sing." Did it sound somewhat unnatural and uncomfortable? Now turn the experiment around and start with "sing" and use that vowel while saying "sit." Do you see what I mean about subtle vowel adjustments?

The vowel chart shown above does not contain both "sit" and "sing" since the difference is subtle. However, once a singer becomes proficient in *gradually* moving through the spectrum of vowel locations, smaller degrees of difference become more vivid.

If you did not sense a difference in vowel sound while saying "sit" and "sing," that doesn't mean you are "wrong," even if most singers tend to focus the two words differently. Singing a given vowel "correctly" is not the point. The purpose here is to explore the full spectrum of vowel sounds in order to make appropriate spontaneous adjustments for the sake of vocal blend. All of this is aimed at preparing singers to match—by ear—the vowel location of any and every variety of singing style and speech dialect.

The Concept "Vowel"

Before learning to identify various vowel locations, one should first learn to isolate the characteristic of vocal sound we call "vowel." As mentioned earlier, vowel is not physically separate from some other vocal characteristics—primarily "brightness." Some vowel sounds are naturally brighter than others, which makes it difficult to demonstrate vowel separate from brightness and vice versa. For now, it will be best to let brightness occur as it will as we focus on vowel locations. Later, we will talk about varying one characteristic without varying the other.

Abstracting separate concepts from the "real world" is not unusual. We do it all the time. For example, in order to see an object, we experience light, color and shadow simultaneously; yet we have little difficulty separating these three concepts for practical reference. That is essentially what we are doing here. By using concepts "vowel" and "brightness" we can learn to focus on each one separately even though vocal sound must contain both in order to exist.

Tongue Position

Experts generally agree that tongue movement is largely responsible for differences in vowel sounds. I remember reading about vowels being "formed in the pharynx," but that idea never made practical sense to me so I will not comment on it. On the other hand, I found the "tongue movement" idea both practical and effective.

Here is a simple exercise to help singers isolate "vowel" from other components. Place one hand lightly around the jaw with the index finger turned upward across the open lips and sing "ah." Then change the vowel to "ee," relying on the hand to help avoid moving the jaw and lips. Notice that the tongue moves up and forward while singing "ee" and then back down into the lower jaw for the return to "ah." Repeat the movement, singing "ah-ee-ah-ee-ah," in order to absorb the physical "feedback" regarding the kind of movement that produces the difference in the sounds "ah" and "ee."

When performing this exercise with a group, singers can practice imitating what they hear around them. At this point, they needn't be concerned about the "correctness" of the vowel (even though in the future a director will likely request specific modifications according to stylistic considerations or personal preferences). A consensus of agreement, even among beginning singers, is usually more than adequate for making the point.

During these early drills, emphasis on listening is important in that the ear is primarily responsible for monitoring vocal adjustments. This makes muscle movement an apparent *result* rather than a cause, thus minimizing vocal tension.

Next, sing "ah-oo-ah," again with the hand monitoring for unwanted lip and jaw movement. In this case, since a natural sounding "oo" requires participation of the lips, one may feel awkward when hearing the rather strange result. At this point, it should be clear that the tongue is largely responsible for vowel focus. Therefore, it is important to avoid moving anything other than the tongue in order to isolate its effect on vowel.

Again, group singers should be encouraged to listen to one another and imitate the group sound no matter how "bad" they consider it. When they hear agreement, they will also realize how it was accomplished. Later, when poor vowel focus appears —particularly on an "oh" or "oo" vowel—the singers will be more likely to examine tongue position as the likely culprit.

Once the role of the tongue is understood in creating vowel focus, the prohibition against lip movement can and should be relaxed. Ultimately, the ear needs to have total freedom to adjust whatever physical element will produce the desired result.

Vowel Location

The vowel chart is a helpful tool for practicing the relative locations of vowel sounds. Now, while pointing to a reference word on the outer rim of the chart, sing its vowel (not the whole word). Then move the pointer to other reference words and sing those vowels. Notice what the tongue does in order to focus each vowel sound. Using a pointer with the chart is helpful, I believe, even when used by a single singer. Moving the pointer helps to reinforce direction and distance in tongue movement, especially for novice singers.

The vowel sound "ah" (father) is a good starting point since it uses an open and relaxed tongue position. By singing such combinations as "ah-a-ah" (father-sat-father), "ah-aw-ah" (father-saw-father) or "ah-i-ah" (father-sit-father), the singer develops a sense of distance and direction. In group sessions, singers can listen to one another and attempt to agree on the location by adjusting their individual sounds.

Once this skill is developed, the terms "front vowel," "back vowel," "high vowel" and "low vowel" have clear and practical meaning. A request by a director to move a vowel "slightly higher" not only can be understood by the singers but now they also have the experience by which to grant the request. When a vowel discrepancy persists, simply reminding singers to listen to one another can frequently solve it. A singer's ear is often able to intuit the solution more easily and clearly than his or her brain is able to understand it "intellectually."

The Most Frequently Misplaced Vowel

I have found that the most difficult vowel sound for singers to locate is the vowel "eh," as in "set." Curiously, many singers who clearly *speak* the vowel do not use it while singing. Instead, they sing a vowel nearer to "sat." When this is sung with other singers who are producing a well placed "eh," the result is rather jarring.

Are you one of those singers? Let's find out. Say aloud the word "Amen." Did your second-syllable vowel match the one in "set"? Now *sing* the word "Amen." Did you sing "A-man" (as in "sat")? If so, try raising your tongue position. If you sang it correctly, you are one of the few singers who do not place it too low.

I suspect that teaching singers to drop the jaw into the "singing position" may have inadvertently caused this common disability. The jaw goes down and the tongue goes with it. That works well for the vowel "ah," but not for the vowel "eh." Evidently, it takes considerable conscious effort to overcome this habit and to separate tongue movement from jaw movement. The hand-on-the-jaw technique (described above) can be a great help in curing this ailment.

Yes, I realize that some may consider this discussion a matter of taste. However, I consider it important that singers *be able* to sing lyrics in a manner corresponding to standard speech. If one *chooses* to perform lyrics differently for singing than for speaking, that is another matter. We will have more to say about that in Chapter 11.

The Missing American Vowel

In many American dialects, the words "sat" and "ask" are pronounced using the same vowel location. Therefore, some singers are confused when they see these two words in different locations on the chart. Standard American broadcast practice, however, places the vowel in "ask" closer to the "ah" in "father."

Dictionaries usually show the "sat" vowel with a "short" mark over the letter "a" and show the "ask" vowel with a dot over the letter "a." The vowel in "father" is usually shown with two dots over the letter "a." To find this "missing" vowel, move slowly between "sat" and "father." The "ask" vowel is located about half way between them. But again, fine-tuning is up to a consensus among the users.

Shades of Vowel

The ultimate solution to these and many other vowel-matching problems lies in developing the ability to produce fine shades of vowel all the way around the outside arc of the chart—from "ee" to "oo" and back again. By *very gradually* changing vowel location between one reference word and a neighboring word, one can learn to fill in those "blank" places (where many singers have never been). A good exercise for developing this skill is to have singers respond to a pointer moving very slowly from one reference word to a neighboring word, filling in the space by gradually sliding vowel location.

During the early stages of learning this skill, some singers "get stuck" on a reference word and then leap suddenly to the neighboring reference word. When that happens, focusing on gradually changing sound—not the reference words themselves—can be helpful. Once the feeling of gradually changing locations is experienced, one can then explore the "missing" vowel area between reference words and experience the physical movements that control those areas.

After successfully filling in all the spaces between reference words, mastery can be demonstrated by moving gradually around the entire periphery of the chart. Begin at "ee" and move gradually through all the shades of vowel around the arc to "ooh." Then move gradually in the other direction starting with "ooh." Be sure that there are no places where the vowel focus jumps from one reference word to the next. Practicing this skill in unison with other singers will help develop the ability to match vowel focus no matter what the language or dialect.

While tongue placement is the primary factor in forming vowel sounds, lips, jaw, and sometimes other mouthparts such as cheeks, are also required for forming some sounds. For example, the umlaut sound used in French and German requires a combination of tongue and lips that does not occur in English. At some point, adjustment of these additional physical factors can also be placed under intuitive control of the ear for fine-tuning. Once the techniques of forming the "easy" vowels are acquired, the groundwork for exploring the less common ones is already in place. At each new step in the process, the singer should continue to be influenced by the aural environment and respond, as in earlier practice, by attempting to match the group sound.

The Neutral Vowel

The portion of the chart inside the arc contains a reference word—sofa (not sofah)—for the "neutral" vowel sound. If you haven't identified this vowel location, you can find it easily by relaxing the face, jaw and tongue, then parting the lips slightly and activating the vocal cords. This sound is the vowel we commonly use for unaccented syllables in speech, as in "portable," "the best," and "gone away." (Say them casually, without exaggerating, or you won't get the point.)

While most people use this sound easily and gracefully in speech, a great many singers exclude it from singing. It is a perfectly good and legitimate vowel (symbolized by an upside-down "e" in the international phonetic alphabet) and its use can add immensely to the rhythmic elegance of a sung phrase. More will be said about this later in the chapter on phrasing, but for now it is sufficient to simply identify and *experience* the neutral vowel—in singing as well as speaking.

Inside Vowels

Three other reference locations appear on the inside area of the chart. "S<u>u</u>ch" can be found below the neutral vowel (toward "f<u>a</u>ther"), "<u>ear</u>th" is up and forward (toward "s<u>ee</u>n") and "t<u>oo</u>k" is up and backward (toward "s<u>oo</u>n"). It is quite worth the effort to locate these areas by isolating tongue movement before modifying them with lips and cheeks. As with the other vowel locations, these are flexible and subject to fine-tuning according to style, taste and ensemble blend.

Mastery

Mastery of vowel skills is evidenced by the ability to move gracefully and with clear focus to any location on the chart, including the spaces between reference words. Application, on the other hand, will require two additional skills: the ability to match by ear any prevailing vowel location produced by one's fellow singers in ensemble, and the ability to modify vowel location when requested by a choral director or vocal coach.

I have found that working with individuals within the group setting is extremely productive. My favorite technique is to establish vowel agreement with two or three singers and then add one singer at a time to the sound. As each singer enters the sound, the group hears the added sound as agreeing or conflicting. When the latter occurs, I identify the problem and suggest the remedy. When the adjustment repairs the disagreement, all have learned something about vowel focus.

Whether to work with individuals or only with the group as a whole is a matter that teachers and directors will have to judge for themselves. However, the likelihood that some singers will not realize they are "offenders" must be considered when making that decision. In my experience, once singers hear the difference that success offers, they are more than willing to make sure they are "doing it right." Fear of being made an example is further minimized when singers have been weaned from the concept "my voice" and have accepted the idea that their voice is a versatile and flexible instrument.

CHAPTER FIVE

Brightness

The vowel spectrum has an inherent natural variation in brightness; for example, "seen" is much brighter than "soon." However, the brightness component can be modulated independently as a separate variable. The vowel can be held constant (largely by maintaining tongue position) while other parts of the vocal apparatus can be modified to vary the brightness.

It is important that singers separate the concepts of vowel and brightness. When asked to raise an incorrect "sat" vowel focus to "set," singers often widen the lips (which brightens the sound) but fail to move the tongue (which would change the vowel focus). The confusion is understandable since "set" is naturally brighter than "sat," but it is evident that these singers do not understand the difference between the two components.

In order to concentrate specifically on brightness, singers must first be secure in their understanding of vowel location and focus. Ill-defined concepts and tentative skills will only lead to increased confusion, both in sound sensitivity and in terminology. Just as learning about musical meter relies on a solid grasp of basic pulse, learning brightness modification is fully dependent on mastering basic vowel focus.

Change in the size and shape of the mouth appears to be the main factor in modifying brightness, however, other factors likely contribute. Knowing the causal functions of all the specific mouth parts is not particularly critical to identifying the brightness variable since the adjustments can be governed directly by what the ear hears. As with the other components, one can learn the "moves" that cause changes in brightness simply by listening to and experimenting with darker and brighter sounds.

The tongue, of course, must remain in the prevailing vowel position in order to isolate changes in the brightness component. As one explores the brightness component in all parts of the vowel spectrum, the concept of brightness becomes more vivid and distinct.

Brightness Drills

It would seem logical to begin brightness drills with the "ah" vowel focus. Since the tongue is basically at rest there, it is easier to maintain the vowel while experimenting with brightness. Once the idea (and the feeling) is secure, other parts of the vowel spectrum can be explored with less likelihood of tongue movement.

Drills can be conducted visually by pointing to reference words on the vowel chart. Sliding the pointer under a reference word can indicate changes in brightness. The singers, of course, must be instructed that the focus of this drill is on brightness, not vowel. As the pointer slides forward (to the left) under a word, singers respond by brightening the sound. As the pointer slides backward (to the right), they darken the sound. In ensemble practice, singers have the added reinforcement of matching the group's sound.

Although these vowel and brightness drills are designed to isolate the two components as separate concepts, keep in mind that the physical sounds of vowel and brightness are not necessarily *acoustically* different. In fact, some vowel sounds are brought into focus using some of the same anatomical adjustments used to create brightness modifications. For example, in order to achieve a well-focused "ooh" vowel, the tongue requires help from the cheeks and mouth. Also, one can move between the "ah" and "aw" vowels by moving *either* the tongue or cheeks. So, there is not a one-to-one relationship between tongue and vowel and between brightness and other mouthparts.

That realization, however, does not invalidate the value of examining the role of the tongue in creating basic vowel focus and the role of other mouthparts in modifying those vowel sounds. Remember that it is the formation of *concepts* that allows us to organize our experiences of physical reality. Consider that "pitch" and "pulse" are essentially made of the same stuff—regularly recurrent physical events—yet we have no difficulty identifying them as very different perceptual concepts.

The point here is that we *think* of vowel and brightness as different concepts, having abstracted those concepts from our experience of physical sound. Our purpose then is simply to experience the anatomical adjustments that produce sound modification appropriate to each separate concept. It is not particularly important to totally analyze every physical movement that produces every sound modification. We can simply leave that up to the ear and its direct connection to the brain to accomplish the job.

Once a singer or ensemble becomes familiar with the technique of modifying vowel with shades of brightness, a world of artistic possibilities is opened. If the mood requires a somber tone, the singers are prepared to deliver well-matched phrases, instinctively adjusting the natural brightness of every vowel in order to present a consistent flow of vocal color. When brighter shades are needed, the singers are equally prepared to create the appropriate sound. Once these skills are honed, it all happens without conscious thought. One's whole attention is devoted to *making music*.

CHAPTER SIX

Resonance

Some singers produce a beautiful, full sound with seemingly little effort, while others produce a dull, lifeless, weak tone, sometimes in spite of great physical effort. The difference is often attributed to "natural talent" (or lack of it) which too often gives the poorer singer reason to accept his or her instrument "as is." After years of struggling with "breath support," "vowel placement," "singing in the mask" and other good practices, many singers still seem unable to break through the barrier that inhibits them from singing with a free and beautiful tone.

Lack of resonance may appear to be a less critical factor than other components in larger choral groups, since poorly resonated vocal sound does not contribute much to the total choral product. The best that can be said for singers lacking resonance is that they "don't get in the way" vocally while helping fill the stage with bodies. Needless to say, social participation has its own reward, but this alone cannot match the satisfaction of actually contributing to an elegant ensemble sound.

On the other hand, singers having poor resonance often resort to shouting when the dynamic level rises. When singers "push" the sound, they not only injure the ensemble's blend but risk injuring their own vocal instrument. Very often, the suggestion offered to such singers is to "support" the sound with good breathing techniques. This advice, while good in itself, can easily lead to *more* tension and simply add to the problem. "Supporting" a poorly resonated tone is largely a wasted effort.

Understanding the nature of "noisy tone" may help to find a cure. Actually, this phrase is an oxymoron, since by definition tone is "regular vibrations" and noise is "irregular vibrations." Poorly resonated loud vocal sound contains considerable "noise," thus blurring pitch (which requires regular vibrations). Also, the tension required to produce noisy sound inhibits vocal flexibility. As a result, such sounds are nearly impossible to tune.

Therefore, "supporting" noise in the tone is counterproductive in the quest for vocal blend. How, then, can a choral director develop a robust and artistically flexible ensemble sound that minimizes vocal noise, maximizes vocal tone and resonates to the farthest reaches of the concert hall with minimal effort?

Seeking Resonance

A likely clue to understanding resonance can be found in a rather unlikely place—the shower. Every shower singer knows that when a certain pitch is sung, the whole room seems to vibrate. On that pitch, the voice is amplified many times louder than on other pitches. Singing with a robust free tone on that particular pitch is easy. The voice sounds *great* with little effort.

When the frequency of sound waves "matches" the dimensions of the shower, the waves reflect off the hard shower wall and arrive back at the source just in time to be in sync with new sound waves just starting out—thus doubling and redoubling the sound. This phenomenon is called *resonance*, or re-sounding,

Fortunately, we don't need to take the shower with us to the concert stage. Actually, we would need an enormous number of showers of different sizes and shapes in order to accommodate the variety of pitch/vowel combinations needed for a performance. Happily, nature has provided us with adjustable "shower walls" within the vocal apparatus. One can learn to control the resonance component automatically, like other components, based on information received by the ear. All that is needed is the *concept* of resonance as remembered from the shower experience and the willingness to explore vocal sounds to discover what adjustments will produce that result.

Unlike the shower, the vocal apparatus changes shape with every variety of pitch/vowel combination. The singers' challenge, then, is to maintain resonant sound while other components change. The singer who produces rich and vibrant tone throughout a performance has discovered (consciously or intuitively) the physical adjustments that cause all combinations of pitch and vowel to sound rich and full without undue physical effort.

Just as physical brightness is not fully separate from physical vowel, physical resonance is not fully separate from physical vowel. Neither is resonance separate from pitch (as one might expect, considering the "shower walls" analogy).

Nevertheless, all of these components can be abstracted and experienced as conceptually separate variables by controlled experimentation. Experiencing the resonance component is most easily accomplished by holding pitch constant and adjusting vowel. This is analogous to varying the "shower walls" instead of the pitch. When resonance "pops" into focus the difference is immediately evident, much like the shower walls experience.

Ringing Vowels

The "lazy" vowels we normally use for everyday speech are not the same as the "energized" ones needed for good singing. Therefore, singers suffering from poor resonance should attempt to explore places in the vowel spectrum they have never visited. As we all know, old habits are persistent, particularly when one has lived with the concept of "my voice" for many years.

While a group approach is probably sufficient for teaching vowel, pitch and other components, teaching resonance is best done individually. Focusing on resonance is difficult for singers who have never experienced it in any way. In fact, some singers may not realize they haven't identified it. For these singers, personal outside input is critical.

In my experience, teaching resonance is most effectively accomplished by demonstration. By hearing a skilled singer move resonance in and out of focus, one can learn what to listen for. The singer can then experiment to discover the "shower walls" adjustment for that same pitch/vowel combination. After finding success with a few different combinations, the singer will discover the process and will find that it can be applied similarly to any pitch/vowel combination.

The resonance "hot spot" is much more evident when singing the "outside" (relative to the chart) vowel sounds, as opposed to the more neutral "inside" vowel sounds. Front vowels (left side of the chart) generally seem to "ring" by moving the focus forward toward (and beyond) the teeth. The sustaining vowel in "say" is a good sound to begin with since it contains considerable natural brightness. Likewise, back vowels (right side of the chart) seem to "ring" when the focus is moved back toward the throat.

Resonance focus can be found in the middle vowels in a similar manner. As with the "outside vowels," the idea is to discover the adjustments that cause these vowels to "ring" in the best possible way. Even the neutral vowel can be significantly enhanced by giving attention to resonance focus, although not nearly as much as the "outside" vowel sounds.

Once these skills are in evidence, singers can explore the challenge of maintaining resonance while changing vowel and pitch—first separately and then together. Eventually, resonance will magnify every combination of pitch and vowel the singer encounters. The payoff can be dramatic.

The ultimate in vocal resonance occurs when a singer is able to imagine the sound existing completely outside the body. At this performance level, the vocal artist is no longer focusing on the details of vocal technique, but rather is totally absorbed in generating and shaping the sound as it fills the auditorium. The experience is quite like sending signals to a radio controlled spacecraft soaring through the heavens.

Can any singer achieve that level of vocal artistry? I don't know, of course. But, I do think it is a goal worth striving for.

CHAPTER SEVEN

Nasality

Like other components, nasality can be adjusted by moving the appropriate vocal muscles. As the air column passes through the throat, it can be directed entirely through the nose by touching the back of the tongue to the soft palate (as when singing "ng"), thus closing off the mouth. By gradually separating the soft palate away from the tongue, increased amounts of air are split off and directed through the mouth. When the soft palate and tongue move to the point where they are farthest apart, nearly all of the flow is directed through the mouth.

Vocal sound is generally rather pleasant when about half the sound is directed toward nasal resonance. From that neutral point, quite a range of musical results are possible by shifting the predominance to either the mouth or nasal cavities. "Correctness" of a particular adjustment is largely a matter of musical taste and style, and like other components is controlled by what the ear wants to hear. A full-throated operatic performer or hard rock vocalist might favor mouth resonance while a typical "bluegrass" singer or jazz artist might favor nasal resonance.

To produce a slick commercial or jazz sound, a vocal group might combine a considerably nasalized mixture (roughly 70%) moderately compressed (using breath support) into a rather straight, vibrato-less tone. For a high gloss "stainless steel" effect, a vocal group might increase nasality to maximum and compress the tone until the individual pitches virtually disappear into the chord.

Background Effects

One of the "secrets" of blending homophonic jazz harmonies is to nasalize the harmony parts in contrast to the lead. While the lead singer, or singers, perform(s) the melody in a more or less solo style, other singers emphasize nasal resonance and compress the tone into a simple "pitch and vowel" sound. This creates a "homogenized" vocal that might be described as a "harmonically-colored melody" a la The Manhattan Transfer, Take Six or The Real Group.

Nasalized resonance is also useful for creating a sustained choral background to solo or soli melodic lines. Instead of singing a normal "ah" or "ooh" (as commonly prescribed in choral scores), it is often effective to neutralize a vowel and warm it by increasing nasal resonance. This provides a natural contrast to the focused vowels and balanced resonance of the melody. Suggesting the singers imitate a synthesizer sound helps them to abandon the normally-focused vowel and to modify it toward a sound appropriate to the musical selection.

The choice of vowel for a background is sometimes key to finding a satisfying musical result. In the L.A. Jazz Choir's recording of Miles Davis's "Blue In Green," the a cappella background to Vicki McClure's haunting solo was largely based on nasalized/neutralized "ooh's" and "ah's." Her final sustained lyric was the word "seems." The "ooh"-based background simply didn't work with that vowel. It shattered the mood and fought with Vicki's sensitive closing. When we changed the background vowel to "ee" and applied appropriate brightness modification, the effect was perfect. I would think one would not normally consider "ee" for use as a background vowel; yet, when warmed by neutralizing and nasal resonance, it worked very nicely.

Another consideration in this regard has to do with choral scores that prescribe humming as a background. A common problem is that closed-mouth humming often does not provide sufficient sound and, when forced, can cause vocal tightness. A practical solution is to sing such passages on the neutral vowel with considerable nasal resonance. In other words, hum with the lips slightly parted. The sound is much more rich and vibrant and vocal freedom is less likely to be constricted. The audience will still hear the passage as humming—but the point is that they *will* hear it.

A Cure-all?

From the previous discussion, one might get the impression that nasality is little more than a means of producing stylistic and artistic color preferences. Actually, this component can be used effectively in a variety of styles for maximizing choral blend. One might even consider it a panacea for a variety of ills.

During my early years as a choral director, I would often struggle with a blend problem—adjusting vowel, fine-tuning pitch, focusing resonance, etc. To my surprise, when I asked the singers to increase the nasal tone and minimize mouth tone, the blend problem disappeared, almost magically.

The reason may be that the nasal passage is less subject to individual singer variations since its shape cannot be manipulated as can the mouth. But whatever the reason, I found that increasing nasality can often be a useful "quick fix" for achieving choral blend, provided that sort of tone is appropriate to the vocal style.

Imagery Does It

Control of this component, like others, is best left to the ear. While it is possible to manipulate the tongue and glottis by direct physical thought, it is always better to use imagery in order to avoid vocal tension. Traditionally, this value has been expressed by the phrase "singing in the mask." Of course, we know that sound does not emanate from the eyes. Yet, imagining that it does helps singers to open the gate to nasal resonance (the soft palate) without really thinking about the physical adjustment needed to accomplish it.

To help singers experience this feeling, ask them to hold an open hand about an inch in front of the mouth, but below the nose, and to "sing over the fence." Since the "fence" would seem to block much of the mouth sounds, singers intuitively direct the energy of the sound "through the eyes." It works very well and the vocal result is usually quite stunning. Once the group gets the idea and hears the result, the "fence" can, of course, be discarded. Thereafter, a simple request for "more eyes," or something similar, should produce the desired result.

CHAPTER EIGHT

Pitch

The phrase "singing in tune" has at least two general meanings. One has to do with melodic tuning—singing pitches one after the other that relate to a single central pitch (sounded or imagined). The other has to do with harmonic tuning—singing related pitches simultaneously with other performers. Despite that distinction, the two are not totally unrelated. Experience with good harmonic tuning very likely contributes to the development of good melodic tuning.

Since vocal tuning in both contexts is relational, the phrase "singing in tune" prompts the question: "Singing in tune with what?" To some singers, the phrase means singing in tune with a piano, or other fixed pitch instrument. To others, the phrase means singing pitches that relate directly to one another regardless of what a keyboard might play. If that distinction comes as a surprise, you may not be aware that the tuning used in our modern keyboards is not the same as nature's tuning.

A Little History

Centuries ago, singers and string players very likely adjusted pitches "on the fly" to fit the harmonic context. When chords and keys changed, they moved their pitches slightly in order to preserve harmonic agreement. When keyboards became an essential part of seventeenth-century music making, a problem arose in that keyboards tuned in one key would have to retune to play in another key. Some attempts were made to add extra strings and digitals; however, this became very cumbersome and was eventually abandoned. Instead, keyboard makers opted for compromised tunings that would allow the keyboard to "get by." Singers and string players largely tuned as before while keyboard players did the best they could.

The Problem

The modern practice of keyboard tuning divides the octave into twelve equal half steps, which distributes the compromise equally among all keys. This solution—called *equal temperament*—was unquestionably a practical one, enabling keyboardists to play in any key without retuning. But the gain to keyboardists has contributed to an unfortunate setback for vocalists. Performing with modern keyboards has taught singers to hear those tunings as "correct," and as a result many singers—even experienced ones—have some difficulty singing in tune with one another.

The problem is magnified when singers "learn their notes" by listening to them played on a keyboard. Commonly, whole sections of choral singers sing their individual parts while the accompanist supplies the *tuning* as well as "the notes." Then, after all sections have practiced in the keyboard's compromised tuning, they sing their learned music together, frequently with little regard for the overall tuning of the combined voices. The long-held assumption has been that, as long as the parts are in tune with the piano, the parts will be in tune with one another.

The reality is that such practice seldom leads to "in tune" choral performances. While keyboards get by with compromised tuning, singers cannot hope to do so. The difference, as I see it, is twofold. First, the well-tuned keyboard's degree of compromise is fixed; it cannot get any better or worse. In contrast, a singer's sense of tuning is constantly subject to correction. Good singers correct well; poor singers are often at sea. Secondly, the keyboard's timbre is also fixed, while vocal tone is continually changing timbre (vowel) as well as other variables.

As a result, a cappella performances by choirs who habitually learn their tuning from a keyboard are potentially disastrous. As soon as the piano withdraws its support, any sense of tonality sinks into oblivion (if indeed it was there before the keyboard stopped playing). In some cases, difficulty maintaining tonality is evident even when the piano is present. For such choirs, tuning is a constant problem and is always tentative and approximate.

Vocal tuning problems inherited from the keyboard's compromise are not limited to choral singers. Many soloists find it uncomfortable to perform without hearing the vocal melody played by the accompanist. Of course, that insecurity often has to do with singing the right pitches, regardless of tuning. A good example of this is the often awkward result when someone with a so-called "good voice" is asked to sing at a friend's wedding. Sadly, many soloists continue to depend on the keyboard's melodic support even after many years of performing. One must only assume that these singers are unaware of the keyboard's tuning limitations.

The Solution

At the other extreme, experienced soloists often request that a keyboardist *not* play the vocal melody, leaving them to sing the melody freely—in regard to both tuning and rhythm. The musical result is often much more expressive. Very likely, these soloist are not only aware of the keyboard's limitations but have developed a level of performance skills that produces secure and artistic tuning.

Let it be clear that the point here is not to denigrate keyboards, rather to suggest that vocalists and choral directors be aware of the tempered-tuned keyboard's inability to produce acoustically true harmonic and melodic tunings. That, of course, raises some obvious questions. Can we adjust our firmly ingrained musical habits to accommodate this information? Can we teach our amateur choirs to sing the "right notes" without playing them on the keyboard? Is it worth the trouble? Is it really that important?

Learning to sing with acoustic tuning is actually not difficult, particularly for novice singers who have few or no "bad" tuning habits to overcome. Some of my professional workshop singers, on the other hand, would appear to be stuck on the "piano fifth," while attempting to tune a perfect fifth (G above C, for example). When asked to raise their fifth until it tunes to a sounding root they appear puzzled and ask, "But aren't I already in tune?" When asked to risk being sharp to see what happens, they begin exploring. After a few attempts to break out of the tempered-tuning habit, they find they are able to slide the pitch up until it "locks" acoustically. Their eyes light up as though they have discovered a new world. The truth is, they have.

Occasionally, one of these explorers would say, "But isn't my pitch now sharp?" My reply would be, "If you mean, 'Is it higher than the pitch you're used to?' the answer is 'yes,' but if you mean, 'Does it acoustically "disagree with" the lower tone,' then the answer is clearly 'no.' The ear tells us it is *in tune.*"

Some Suggestions

Here are some ideas for demonstrating what acoustic tuning sounds and feels like. It is important to begin with basic tuning at the unison. This concept is usually quickly evident since it is not unlike what singers learn to do while imitating keyboard models. Play or sing a single sustained tone (without vibrato) and slowly move another voice in and out of tune with it. The perceivable difference between the "in tune" condition (smooth and agreeable) and the "out of tune" condition (rough and disagreeable) is usually vivid.

Invite individual singers to perform the demonstration to ensure that all grasp the idea and the skill. Eventually, have all the singers together tune to various model pitches, tuning instantly to each new pitch. For this exercise, it is not important that the model pitches be "in tune" melodically with previous model pitches. In fact, it is probably better if they are not, requiring the singers to listen carefully to the model pitch itself, not to any imagined harmonic context.

Always match timbre while performing these demonstrations. When using a voice or voices as the model pitch, have the moving voice use the same vowel or humming tone. If using an electric keyboard or organ for the model pitch, select a flute or string sound if possible and ask the singer to imitate that timbre. If using a piano, ask the player to re-strike the tone frequently to simulate a sustained sound, and have the moving voice match it by singing a nasalized neutral vowel

A good transitional exercise for harmonic tuning is to practice singing octaves. Octaves, of course, are commonly thought of as "the same pitch" higher or lower. In this exercise, play or sing a sustained low pitch and slowly move another voice in and out of tune with it at a pitch one or more octaves higher. This is only slightly more challenging than the unison drill, and is usually accomplished with very little additional practice.

Thanks to nature's gift of harmonic perception, the same tuning discrimination can be experienced when two *different* (but acoustically related) pitches are performed "in tune" and "out of tune." By making the same adjustments experienced in the unison and octave tuning exercise, one can learn to locate accurate tuning of harmonically related pitches.

The next most consonant (harmonically agreeable) interval after the octave is the perfect fifth. Therefore, it is the logical one to practice next. Like the unison and octave drills, the area just outside of the "in tune" focus is quite noisy, or dissonant. Therefore, it is almost as easy to perceive accurate tuning of the fifth as it is the tuning of the unison and octave. The perfect fourth, which is the inversion of the perfect fifth (G-C, for example), is the next most consonant interval.

The next most consonant set of intervals is the major third and its inversion, the minor sixth. Tuning these intervals is somewhat less obvious to the ear than the fifth/fourth set. Nevertheless, the idea is the same as before—to simply locate the tuning that seems most "locked." Likewise for the next set of intervals—the minor third and major sixth.

Next, tune the combined three pitches that constitute the major triad (for example, C-E-G). These three pitches occur "naturally" as a root, fifth and major third in the acoustic partials series, therefore they are quite easy to tune, even by beginners.

With practice, even the more dissonant major and minor sevenths and seconds can be experienced as locked intonations. Eventually, four-note chords can be tuned acoustically. At each stage, the principle is the same—to listen for the adjustments that cause the pitches to sound most in agreement.

Retuning "On the Fly"

While tuning by ear is simple in principle, it is important to realize that as harmonic contexts change during the course of a musical composition, the optimal tuning of individual pitches is likely to change as well. For example, scale step 4 (F in the key of C) tuned in the context of a IV chord (F-A-C) will change to a considerably lower pitch when tuned in the context of a V7 chord (G-B-D-F).

Fortunately, knowing the theory is *not* required for successful spontaneous tuning. Simply keeping one's ear vigilant to locate the "best" adjustment for every prevailing context will do the job very nicely. Obviously, these adjustments are best made without a keyboard's help. On the other hand, having a keyboard play roots (only) may help singers hear where adjustments of chord members should be placed.

(If you would like to know more about these kinds of exercises, our publications *Natural Ear Training* and *The Sounds of Music: Perception and Notation* elaborate on the topic. Ordering information can be found in the final pages of this book.)

Warm-ups Without a Keyboard

Because tempered tuning habits are so strong in our general musical environment, a tuning warm-up exercise at the beginning of every rehearsal is essential to remind singers to use acoustic tuning. For example, have half the singers sustain a reference pitch, and the other half move on cue, slowly and carefully, up and down a major scale, acoustically tuning each scale step before moving to the next. Signal when to move and in what direction, constantly monitoring success and repeating steps that need more attention. Then shift responsibilities by having the other half of the group provide the sustained reference pitch.

Such exercises develop a sense of accurate scale-step intervals and demonstrate how *very small* the half steps are between 3-4 and 7-1 in the major mode. By using this information while singing melodically, not only will chords be more in tune, but melodies (both soli and solo) will take on a new freshness and sparkle. The difference is really quite remarkable.

Consider that the location of the half steps is the identifying feature of any tonality. A singer who has learned to hear and recognize half steps is well on the way to developing a strong sense of tonality and harmonic function. Not a bad payoff for a simple exercise, I would say

Here is an exercise for practicing flexible tuning while moving from one chord to another. One's signals might be as simple as a hand signal indicating a "I" chord by holding up one finger or a "V" chord by holding up five fingers. That, of course, requires that the singers know which scale steps are contained in which chord—information that is not difficult to supply. Alternatively, one might show the scale steps contained in each primary chord on a blackboard or projection screen and point to the chord to be sung and tuned. In the early stages, the basses should always sing roots. (The charts in "Natural Ear Training" are well suited for this purpose.)

Rehearsal Tuning Techniques

In rehearsal, it is often helpful to sustain important chords out of rhythm (and without keyboard assistance), giving singers ample opportunity to explore pitch adjustments. In chordal passages, where all the singers sing the same syllables at the same time, this technique is easily applied by simply gesturing when to change to the next syllable. In contrapuntal passages, pausing at various positions within the conducting beat pattern will work, provided the singers are familiar with rhythm notation. In mixed texture passages, occasional passing tones can be cued with left hand gestures, provided the singers observe the entire score in order to know when *not* to move.

Finally, allow singers sufficient time during rehearsals to "season" their tuning choices. Repeat chromatic passages suffi-ciently enough until the harmonic focus is so sparkling that the listener will be compelled to follow the harmonic logic. Even non-musicians can perceive sparkling intonation, even when they don't realize what they are hearing. At the very least, an audience will notice that there is something very different and exciting about the performance.

Meanwhile, Back at the Keyboard

One other point should be mentioned before leaving this topic. In answer to one of the most "frequently asked questions," it is not a problem to use piano accompaniment to support well-tuned singing provided the pianist does not literally duplicate the pitches being sung. Since the sound of a piano, acoustic guitar or harp decays in loudness, these do not interfere with the sustained sound of voices. On the other hand, when accompanied by an organ, singers should tune to the instrument, particularly when performing purely homophonic music such as a Bach chorale. It is most important to be aware of and well practiced in acoustic tuning and to use good judgment regarding its application.

Having excellent tuning skills is probably the most vital asset a singer can possess. I'm not talking about singing "right notes," but rather the ability to adjust those right notes harmonically when performing in ensemble and to use pitch creatively for expressive solo singing. When a choral group is largely comprised of such singers—be they amateur or professional—there is seldom concern about "going flat." That leaves the performers free to concentrate on producing expressive music.

CHAPTER NINE

Density

"Density" is used here to mean the amount of breathiness in the tone. The full spectrum of density ranges between a closed glottis (*no* air and no phonated sound) and a completely open glottis (*all* air and no phonated sound). A skillful singer moves through that range by adjusting the glottal and breathing muscles.

As with other vocal variables, density adjustments are best controlled by automatic responses to what the ear wants to hear rather than by direct voluntary muscle control. This helps to minimize tension and avoid vocal fatigue or injury.

Many singers perform with one shade of density—commonly a pleasing one, but sometimes with a tone too breathy or too tight for general use. While the main purpose of this discussion has to do with developing *flexibility* in density for artistic use, exploring this component should provide insight for singers whose tone suffers from either "breathiness" or "necktie tone,"

In order to explore density in singing, it is important to understand—or more precisely, to get the feel of—the relationship between the breath and the glottis. To demonstrate this relationship, ask the singers to say very vigorously, "huck-huck-huck," not exploding the final consonant, but instead stopping the sound by containing the breath against the closed tongue and soft palate. Then, ask them to do it again with the tongue relaxed, stopping the airflow further back in the throat. While maintaining the breath pressure, have them move the tongue freely, thus giving evidence that it is the glottis that is stopping the sound.

Next, ask the singers to relax (open) the glottis *very gradually* until it begins to vibrate, first with a thin, crackling sound, then progressively through shades of singing tone and ultimately to a toneless flow of air. Once this is successfully accomplished, singers can go on to explore the sound and feel of various shades of density.

Indirect control of this component can be practiced by asking one singer to perform a melodic phrase using various shades of density and asking other singers to match it. Artistic application of this component can be practiced by asking a singer (or singers) to apply appropriate amounts of density to various phrases having contrasting emotional meaning. For example, the lyric "down with the enemy" would likely be sung with far more density than the phrase "fairer than the loveliest rose."

Of course, such contrasting phrases are likely to be sung with different loudness as well as with different density. To ensure that the variable being practiced is density and not loudness, it might be helpful to sing the phrases alternately with "inappropriate" loudness and density.

With sufficient experimentation and practice, one can learn to control density and apply it as needed. This skill will not only help singers match the sounds of other singers in ensemble, but will also help them modify vocal sounds for artistic and stylistic expression—both in ensemble and in solo performance.

CHAPTER TEN

Loudness

I once considered loudness to be the most critical factor in maintaining choral blend, and would attempt to quiet stronger voices to prevent them from "sticking out." I now believe that loudness is actually one of the least important factors in creating choral blend. In fact, singers who sing too timidly probably injure the blend as often as those who sing too loudly.

As long as a section of singers blends in regard to pitch, vowel, brightness, density, etc., it doesn't much matter if some individual singers are slightly louder than others. Loudness matters only insofar as a section of blended singers relates to another section of blended singers, in which case it becomes a matter of the director's artistic judgment of musical balance.

That point of view, however, does not offer a license for louder singers to "take the lead" and to dominate the sound within a section. The common practice of hiring "paid soloists" to help bolster a local church choir should not create a solo quartet battling it out on Sunday mornings for vocal supremacy. In such choirs, the "average" singers might just as well join the congregation.

The main problem with the overly loud singer is that he or she can't hear the characteristics of the prevailing blend. It goes without saying that a singer who intends to blend must of necessity hear what he or she is attempting to blend *with*. The logical standard then is to sing no louder than will allow for good listening. That will not in itself provide for good blend, but at least it will provide for its possibility.

From the individual singer's point of view, the goal is to match the consensus of sound by adjusting the variables discussed above until one's own voice virtually disappears into it. However, singing more quietly won't disguise a poorly focused vowel or forgive an under-pitch third. All singers must be committed to maintaining all components of the prevailing vocal blend or the sound will be injured, no matter how quietly the wound is inflicted.

It is true, concerning loudness, that not all singers are created equal. Some voices are simply louder than others. While a naturally loud singer can adjust to a softer sound level, the naturally soft singer cannot always increase the sound to match that of the group. As noted above, this is not necessarily a problem. However, as mentioned in Chapter 6, improving his or her skills in resonance can increase a singer's vocal power. There is no reason for a "naturally" small voice to be totally left out of grand climaxes.

On the other hand, it is important to remember that shouting during a loud passage in music does not contribute positively to its impact. Spewing raw emotion may inspire a football team, but it does nothing toward expressing artistic meaning in choral performances. Raucous tone breaks the continuity and mood of a musical expression, offending the sound and diminishing its emotional impact on the listener.

Musical variations in loudness are referred to as "dynamics"—literally "in motion," or "changes." The word is well suited, I believe. It is the changes and nuances in our life experiences that lend meaning to our human existence. Likewise, it is largely the dynamics in an effective musical performance that move us to respond with emotion.

CHAPTER ELEVEN
Phrasing

One might consider phrasing to be outside the topic of vocal blend, having more to do with style and interpretation. However, elegant phrasing requires that all ensemble members are equipped to produce it, and in that sense, phrasing is just as important to vocal blend as any of the topics previously discussed.

Vocal phrasing involves more than simply deciding where to breathe. Well-formed and rhythmic phrasing infuses life into music. Consider the difference in viewing a flat horizon or viewing the contours of a majestic mountain range. In the latter, the eye is invited to explore the energy of the sight, moving rhythmically over the foothills, metaphorically struggling up the steep slopes and relaxing gracefully into the valleys.

That aspect of phrasing, however, is shared by both vocal and instrumental performance and is not the primary focus of this discussion. Vocal phrasing has another dimension. In addition to the general contour and energy of a phrase, singers access the "nooks and crannies" of phrasing by means of lyrics. This added dimension can be either an asset or a liability, depending on how singers treat it.

A Singer's Most Expressive Tool

Natural speech, particularly in languages of the Western world, contains accents and un-accents that enhance its intelligibility. When lyrics are sung with the natural flow of speech, the audience more easily understands them. On the other hand, when lyrics are sung like a train of boxcars (all syllables having equal stress), listeners are less likely to comprehend them.

I am reminded of a Midwestern university that proudly sings all of its opera performances in English. Ironically, the lyrics are often no more intelligible than if they were sung in their original language. When every syllable is fired at the audience with the same intensity, the result is aural confusion. Sadly, many choral performances are presented this way, thereby preventing the audience from enjoying the full impact of the lyrics.

Perhaps an even more important benefit of singing lyrics in a natural way is the internal rhythm that is brought to the phrase. When sung with natural speech inflections, a phrase takes on a kind of "third dimension" of artistic beauty. When a lyric is sung gracefully, the music itself becomes more attractive and alive.

The factor that provides this added dimension—as it does in all artistic endeavors—is contrast. One level of contrast results from the kaleidoscope of vowel colors inherent in words themselves. This level is very important to the poet who chooses words not only for their literal meanings but also for their sounds. "The Bells," by Edgar Allen Poe, is an excellent example of this concept.

Natural Speech Rhythms

Another level—and likely a more important one rhythmically—is created by stressed and unstressed syllables. This has little or nothing to do directly with syllables occurring on a strong or weak metric beat. Rather, it has to do with neutralizing vowels in appropriate places as suggested by the natural flow of language.

When we speak, we accomplish this without thinking. When speaking the phrase "go to the store," we commonly say "go t' th' store." We don't actually leave out the unaccented vowels; we simply "neutralize" them. (See page 20.)

However, many singers use different modes of language for speaking and singing, imposing a "dah-dah-dah" character on the music that sounds very much like a second grader reading aloud. Such singers ignore the neutralized vowels they use very naturally in normal speech, replacing "go t' th' store" with "go too thah store."

So, What's the Problem?

Why do so many singers distort the language? A number of possibilities come to mind. First, consider the suggestion commonly given to voice students to open the mouth (two fingers wide, as I remember) while singing. This advice may be appropriate, up to a point. But rigidly maintaining a wide-open singing position leads to distorted vowels, lifeless phrasing, unintelligible lyrics and ultimately boring music. Even more offensive is phrasing in which the jaw pops down on every syllable like a ventriloquist's dummy.

Another possible reason that singers perform wooden phrases is that they frequently learn their music imitating the sounds of a rehearsal piano "thumping out" their notes. By the time the concert arrives, these lifeless phrasing habits are well engrained, leaving little hope of natural lyric phrasing. Multiply this practice by years of experience, multitudes of singers, generations of teachers, and it is fairly evident that imitating piano sound—which cannot possibly allow for neutralized vowels—contributes to ugly vocal phrasing.

Somewhat surprisingly, it appears that some singers actually believe they sometimes *should* sing lyrics without neutralizing unstressed vowels. In a vocal jazz workshop, after achieving a particularly well-shaped phrase by means of neutralizing unaccented syllables, a singer remarked on how different jazz phrasing is from classical phrasing. As you might expect, I capitalized on this opportunity and took a moment to demonstrate elegant phrasing in a number of "classical" styles. Unfortunately, too many singers assume they are expected to sing classical music in a stiff and lifeless manner.

Could this be why so many people refuse to attend "boring" choral concerts? May I suggest this is why classical performances are often attractive only to a few historically minded devotees who feel compelled to "keep it alive." When music of any style is performed in a vital and dynamic manner it will come to life, appealing to larger and more enthusiastic audiences.

To be sure, certain historical performance practices dictate traditions such as terraced dynamics, evenness of scale and the like. But consider that Bach and Handel could not have played a crescendo or an accent if they had wanted to, since keyboard instruments then were not capable of doing so. Singers and string players, who could easily have done so, followed the keyboard's lead and simply did not do it.

No doubt singers were influenced by instrumental styles in those days as they are today, but then we don't know for sure that some lyrically sensitive singers *didn't* sing "hah l' loo y'" rather than "hah lay loo yah." In any case, today's performances of period choral music *can* be brought to life by neutralizing the vowels in unaccented syllables.

It's Not a Matter of Loudness

It is important to realize that a neutralized syllable need not be sung softer than other syllables. The effect occurs as naturally in singing as it does in speaking. Because the mouth cavity is smaller when producing a neutralized vowel sound, it does not resonate as loudly as normally focused vowels. Thus, singers need not attempt to sing neutral vowels quieter. They simply *are* quieter. This allows the singer to maintain energy throughout a phrase with steady breath support, an important element in producing artistic and emotional phrasing.

One other point on this topic may be helpful. It has to do with singing neutralized vowels that occur on the highest pitch in a phrase. There is a tendency to sing higher-pitched syllables with a focused vowel rather than a neutralized one, even by singers who generally understand the value of neutralizing. Consider the phrase contained in the song *Over the Rainbow* on the lyric "once in a lullaby." The tendency to sing "lul lah by" with a stressed middle syllable may seem practical in order to fully execute the arch of the phrase, however, one might find it more elegant to neutralize it, treating the high pitch as an embellishment of the preceding pitch ("lul") that is on its way downward to the final pitch ("by").

Returning to the topic of vocal blend, when one or a few singers fail to neutralize, they nullify any elegant phrasing sung by the rest of the group. Because artistic phrasing has more to do with unaccents (neutral vowels) than with accents, the louder open vowels of a few can obliterate the quieter neutralized vowels of the others. In order to maintain the integrity of a well-blended ensemble it is essential that *all* singers be aware of and sensitive to uniform phrasing.

CHAPTER TWELVE

Consensus

"Attitude" is unquestionably an important component of vocal blend. Without singers who agree to strive for vocal blend, there is little chance of achieving it. Every singer must constantly be aware of the consensus of sound in the ensemble and adjust to it, regardless of their personal preferences. Lacking that, producing vocal blend is unlikely.

While that goal may appear logical and practical, there are some commonplace obstacles that can impede consensus. One of these can be the professional singer brought into the group to give substance to the sound. It is certainly desirable to have some trained singers in an amateur ensemble, but it can be a mixed blessing when such singers are unprepared to modify their sounds in the interest of vocal blend. You may remember the previous discussion regarding the many experienced singers who had little prior knowledge of the concepts taught in the L.A. Jazz Choir workshop. It would be a mistake to assume that a hired professsional would automatically know or practice the skills described in this book.

Another commonplace impediment to consensus can be the average singer's concept of "my voice," described earlier. This psychological limitation can inhibit a novice singer just as much as "training" can inhibit an experienced one. Vocal habits are often very persistent and can easily become part and parcel of one's vocal self-image. Frequently, this concept is perpetuated by the assumption that change is not necessary or possible.

We noted earlier that some singers, after having spent small fortunes on vocal training, feel that modification for the sake of blend would compromise the integrity of their training. They also may believe that since their own sound is already well-produced, other singers should be the ones to make any needed modi-fications. There is considerable truth to this argument, and directors themselves often take it for granted when they hire professional singers to perform as section leaders.

Discovering Common Ground

Frequently, such conflicts can be resolved by clarifying the nature of vocal blend and the specific skills needed to achieve it. When a trained singer understands that modifications leading to choral blend are well within the boundaries of healthy vocal production, he or she may be more amenable to exploring them. On the other hand, the refusal or inability of a singer to explore blend components will ultimately render ensemble blend impossible. It really is a matter of all or nothing. Faced with this situation, a director will need to make the hard decision.

In this regard, a director interviewing professional singers for a section leader position would do well to explore a candidate's flexibility regarding vocal styles before hiring. A candidate showing tonal flexibility and sensitivity can't help but become a positive influence on the ensemble's style and blend. Such a singer will provide an excellent model for other section members to emulate.

Actually, these problems tend to disappear painlessly when such singers are persuaded to explore the components of vocal blend. Gradually, singers discover that the various skills required to improve vocal blend are the same skills that improve vocal production. It also becomes evident that these skills are achievable by the average person and are not limited to an elite few. These realizations, combined with a conscious effort to emulate the good tone of other singers, will open up a whole new horizon of vocal versatility and artistic satisfaction. Eventually, the limiting concept of "my voice" is replaced by the liberating idea of "my voices."

Logically, singers agreeing to strive for vocal blend sometimes have to modify some aspect of a vocal habit. Often, what singers give up in order to blend is the noisy part of their tone, sometimes referred to as an "edge." Some soloists tend to like this sound because it gives the voice individuality and carrying power, particularly when performing in a Broadway style. In some cases, an impressively rich or distinctive vibrato must be temporarily relinquished for the sake of the sound. Any extraneous quality that is not shared by the other singers in the ensemble should be surrendered in order to create vocal blend.

On the other hand, a choral group might choose to collectively incorporate any of these distinctive qualities in order to produce a particular style or vocal effect. Again, the requirement is that *all* singers produce it. The director, of course, must decide when a particular vocal quality is appropriate and whether it is consistent with healthy vocal production.

Thousands of fine choral organizations offer extensive evidence that a mix of trained and average voices can produce well-blended choral sounds. Excellent singers need not compromise vocal integrity and average singers need not detract from an artistic product when all agree on vowel, brightness, pitch, etc. As stated earlier, it is not so much the difference in vocal training that prevents vocal blend, but rather the mutual disregard for blend and the lack of technique necessary to achieve it.

The younger the choir members, the less likely that conflicting preconceived notions will inhibit consensus. Vocal habits are less fixed, and a willingness to explore ways of improving the group's sound is more or less a given (provided the teacher secures the children's attention). This flexibility suggests that younger singing groups, given sufficient rehearsal time and talented direction, are likely to acquire the skills of good vocal blend more readily than most adult choirs.

In my own experience, I have found that my entry-level non-auditioned college choir members (mostly beginners) tend to learn the skills of vocal blend more effortlessly than my auditioned chamber singers (mostly experienced singers). Some degree of "rethinking" is usually required in the advanced group. As you realistically evaluate your own situation, perhaps this will help you to plan an approach that will ensure success with your singers.

Agreement of Goals

It is critical to determine whether your singers are striving to achieve true choral excellence or whether they are participating just for "recreation" or "fun." If most of them are in the latter category, you may have a real sales job on your hands. But as you continue to demonstrate what can be achieved if they keep an open mind and apply these vocal concepts, the group will eventually arrive at consensus as it realizes its potential and gets a taste of success.

In a sense, consensus in choral singing is like consensus in a democratic society in which citizens at times agree to relinquish parts of their own individuality for the common good of the group. Only by consensus can certain mutually beneficial goals be reached, both social and artistic. And in both cases, these goals are more pleasantly and effectively achieved when the consensus is voluntary.

So, whatever the experience level and overall goals of your choral ensemble, I wish you well in your pursuit of improved vocal blend, should you decide to undertake the challenge. I also hope some of the ideas contained in this book will prove of value to you in that pursuit. Keep in mind that while fine orchestras, bands and other instrumental groups often thrill audiences with moving performances, nothing compares to the intrinsic human emotional response to beautiful voices artistically combined in concert.

Addendum

Expressive Tuning

Far too many singers believe that performing the "right notes" is the ultimate goal of accurate singing, particularly those who model their tuning on the keyboard. That belief inevitably prevents them from taking advantage of one of the most expressive elements in musical performance—namely, *flexible tuning.* Since traditional music education has largely fixated on the "twelve tones" of the modern keyboard, many, if not most, singers never consider flexible tuning as an expressive element.

Some singers have so much trouble finding the piano's version of the twelve scale steps that they are content to accept any pitch that is in the vicinity. This is not surprising, since *hearing* the "system" of piano pitch is far more difficult than discovering nature's system of tuning.

Artistic Meaning

Whatever the art form, meaning is achieved through the artistic control of continuity and contrast. In musical tuning, the process operates in terms of expectation (the listener's) and deviation (the performer's). That should not suggest that sloppy intonation is therefore artistic. On the contrary, an artistic singer is obliged to establish a continuity of accurate tuning in order for an expressive (deviant) pitch to be heard in contrast to it.

This expressive performance technique can be successfully practiced whether a singer prefers keyboard or natural tuning. The essential elements remain the same—establishing tonal continuity and then adjusting selected pitches for expressive meaning. As you might expect, I prefer that the tonality be established in natural tuning since that continuity is far easier for listeners to apprehend, therefore enhancing the contrast of any modified tunings. Equal tempered tunings are *perceptually* imprecise and therefore provide a less clear basis for contrast

Actually, natural tuning is itself in meaningful contrast to the prevalence (continuity) of keyboard-based tuning. The characterless nature of equal half steps pales when compared to the sparkling relationships of *real* perfect fifths and fourths, for example. Even the novice listener can sense something special when a singer's pitches relate to one another harmonically in a perceptibly cohesive manner.

Common Practices of Flexible Tuning

Perhaps the most frequently heard example of expressive tuning is the "blue" note. There is some difference of opinion as to whether the blue third is properly performed slightly lower than the minor third or slightly higher (between the major and minor thirds). While I prefer the former, it really doesn't make much difference in this discussion, since either one represents a deviation from "normal" thirds. In the opening phrase of *Saint Louis Blues* ("I hate to see…") one might hear both types: the higher on the word "I" and the lower on the word "to."

A blue note appears in two or three places in traditional blues styles: in blue-third relationships to the tonic ($1\text{-}\flat3$), to the dominant ($5\text{-}\flat7$) and to the blue third itself (roughly $\flat3\text{-}\flat5$). In some cases, the blues style includes "raised" pitches that lean upward into a more stable target note, such as the "grace note" $^{\sharp}2$ sliding upward on the word "I" in the example above. Although the piano would have to use the same digital to play these notes, a singer can adjust them according to their different contexts.

The amount of "blueness" (deviation) is, of course, up to the performer's artistic taste. While transcribing music as a forensic musicologist, I have heard blue thirds performed so low that they are closer to the scale step below than to the normal minor third. In one case, a colleague insisted that his "perfect-pitched" assistant preferred calling the note in question a second scale step instead of a blue third. I felt, given the blues nature of the song and the pentatonic characteristic of the melody, that it was simply a very low blue third.

Another common deviation from "expected" tuning is the *high third*. Many experienced singers and string players commonly perform the major third (of a major chord) somewhat higher than in both acoustic and tempered-tuning. I observed quite early that "my" major third was clearly higher than the keyboard's and I assumed that I was simply hearing the acoustic third. I had been teaching college music for several years before I discovered that the acoustic major third is actually *lower* than the keyboard's version.

This shocking news prompted me to research the matter to try to find out why so many musicians seem to favor the high third. After much effort, including the help of a group of on-line microtonalists, the matter is still a mystery. Is the high third caused by some psychoacoustic phenomenon or is it simply a matter of personal taste, perhaps used to "brighten" certain major chords? (For further discussion, go to www.stage3music.com and click on "Mystery of the High Third.")

Like the blue note, this deviation tends to appear in specific scale locations in the performance of major/minor music. Perhaps the most prominent place is on final tonic major chords, particularly loud and climactic ones. In this case, the deviation is applied to scale step 3, creating brilliance and excitement.

The high third also frequently appears in the dominant chord, emphasizing the magnetic pull of the leading tone (scale step 7) toward the tonic. When the dominant seventh pitch (scale step 4) is also present, the "squeezed" (or "stretched," depending on the inversion) tritone combination creates an even more urgent drive toward resolution.

Interestingly, these common tuning deviations are often performed by singers who have not given much thought to flexible tuning. It seems unlikely that directors of amateur choral groups commonly ask their singers to raise major thirds. Evidently, the practice can be instinctive, given appropriate musical contexts. In my experience, I have found this to be the case.

Guidelines for Flexible Melodic Tuning

Which is higher in pitch—$F^\#$ or $G^\flat$? Keyboardists, of course, need not be concerned. Singers, on the other hand, can gain considerable artistic advantage by exploring this question. To my surprise, I found that my microtonalist friends were quite unanimous in agreeing that $G^\flat$, being a variant of G, was closer to G; and $F^\#$ is closer to F. To me, this arrangement is arbitrary and probably has little to do with the expressive performance of major/minor music.

In contrast to that view, I tend to agree with the great cellist Pablo Casals, who taught his students to "lean" an accidental toward its destination (or sponsoring) pitch. More specifically, a raised chromatic note is generally more expressive when tuned closer to the next higher scale step and a lowered chromatic note is generally more expressive when tuned closer to the next lower scale step. It follows, then, that a well-tuned $F^\#$ would be considerably higher then a well-tuned $G^\flat$.

The chromatic upper or lower neighbor is one context in which this tuning principle can be applied. For example, the opening phrase of the song *Beautiful Dreamer* offers two such opportunities for bringing freshness and life to the melody.

Beau - ti - ful Dream - er, wake un - to me.

In this context, the B (even though it is a "regular" scale step) can be tuned as a chromatic lower neighbor to the repeated C. In that sense, the lower neighbor D-$C^\#$-D figure heard a few notes later can be considered a reflection of the C-B-C figure. By tuning both lower neighbors just *slightly* below their sponsoring pitches (in contrast to a keyboard half step), the melody floats over the accompaniment with a fresh elegance.

The emotional first phrase of Franz Schubert's famous *Serenade* can be made even more so by tuning the opening upper chromatic neighbor closer to the sponsoring pitch.

Adjusting the tuning of chromatic appoggiaturas often enhances the elegance of an expressive phrase. The title phrase in *Maria* from Leonard Bernstein's "Westside Story" offers a case in point.

The F$^{\#}$, when tuned closely to the target G, enhances the expressive lyric much more than a keyboard half step could ever dream of doing.

Modulatory chromatics are often expressively enhanced by adjusting their tuning toward the destination pitch. In a real sense, higher chromatic leading tones (scale step 7) serve to point the listener toward the new (or temporary) key. Similarly, lowered dominant seventh pitches (scale step 4) can reinforce the energy of the dominant function.

The main reason these tuning adjustments enhance tonality is that the tritone relationship (between scale steps 7 and 4) constitutes the "motor" that drives tonal relations in major/minor music. By enhancing that energy through adjusted tuning, the possibilities for creating exciting music are increased many times over.

(For further discussion of the tritone's role in helping to define and shape tonality, see the *The Sounds of Music: Perception and*

Notation or *Lies My Music Teacher Told Me*, both offered by Stage 3 Publishing.)

Guidelines for Flexible Harmonic Tuning

As chords and keys change in the course of a choral composition, optimum natural tuning of "notes" changes as well. The "A" in an F chord does not tune the same as an "A" in a G9 chord or in a C6 chord. Not only does the "A" adjust to a different root in each case but to every other pitch in that chord as well.

In my first book, *Lies My Music Teacher Told Me*, I suggested that the ear naturally senses acoustic consonance of small-number ratios and can guide the voice to emulate those relationships. Perhaps the most vivid example of this process is the difference in tuning of scale step 4 (F in the key of C) in the contexts of a subdominant chord and a dominant seventh chord.

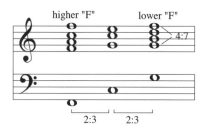

In the subdominant chord, tuning the "F" is largely determined by its relationship to the tonic C—a perfect fifth 2:3 ratio. In the dominant seventh chord, tuning the "F" is largely determined by its relationship to the dominant root G—a "small" minor seventh 4:7 ratio.

To experience this tuning difference, try singing this simple exercise. First, play a C root in bass range and sing a well-tuned major third (E) an octave or two above it. From this tuning, alternately move to the two different tunings of "F." Play the root in each case in order to tune the voice to it. As you will hear, moving to the dominant seventh chord (G root) requires a very small adjustment to the "F," while moving to the subdominant chord (F root) requires a much larger adjustment.

This difference in tuning is even more vivid when the roots are sung rather than played on a keyboard. A fine-tuning exercise such as this is an excellent warm-up for choral rehearsals and helps to remind singers to tune flexibly.

Another example of flexible tuning is to observe the influence of major and minor thirds on the tuning of a chord seventh.

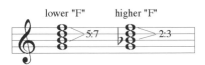

When the third of the chord is major, the natural acoustics of the pitch relationships (4:5:6:7) influence the seventh to be sung lower, emphasizing the active nature of the tritone (5:7). When the third of the chord is minor, there is no tritone. In this case the chord seventh tunes to the minor third as a perfect fifth (2:3 ratio) resulting in a higher tuning of the seventh.

Let me emphasize that pitch-sensitive singers may know little or nothing about math, yet they can still take advantage of flexible tuning. No matter how complex the chord, the ear guides the singer to the "best possible" adjustment of the pitch. The process is not unlike a photographer adjusting focus in order to achieve the sharpest image possible.

Teaching Expressive Tuning

The design of the human auditory system is quite remarkable. To take full advantage of it, a singer must be aware (consciously or intuitively) that vocal tuning is not achieved by matching the keyboard's pitches. Given the chance, the ear will import and process the information—first by example, and then by experimentation.

Nevertheless, formal music education, as commonly practiced, often frustrates this natural process. Playing singers' "notes" on a keyboard is probably the most troubling practice in this regard. Educators might instead develop techniques that provide experiences whereby their singers can discover for themselves natural and expressive vocal tuning

For more information and suggestions for learning and teaching these skills, see "Natural Ear Training" on our website at www.stage3music.com. Click on "Publishing," then on "Natural Ear Training." This publication is *not* a sight-singing method. In fact, it does not require music reading. It is simply designed to help music students experience well-tuned pitch relationships.

Once the *sounds* of well-tuned harmonic and melodic structures become familiar and habitual, the task of applying that information to notation is infinitely easier and, as a result, more meaningful. It is as logical as learning to *speak* a language before learning to read and write it. The big payoff, of course, is that tuning then can become a significant element in an artistic vocal performance.

NATURAL **EAR TRAINING**

For developing basic concepts of
- **Pitch relations**
- **Acoustic tuning**
- **Harmonic structures**
- **Chord connections**
- **Melodic principles**

The value of a natural approach to ear training is immediately evident to anyone who realizes that keyboards cannot accurately reproduce pitch relations in the same way that ears hear them. While the keyboard is limited to one tuning per digital, the sensitive musical ear naturally tends to adjust tuning according to the harmonic and melodic context of pitches. It follows then that any approach to developing musical aural skills should focus on the nature of relative pitch perception and avoid the compromised sound models produced on a keyboard.

Our current fascination with digital electronics and computerized teaching methods tends to distract us from a natural perception of pitch relations. In my experience, accurate acoustic tuning cannot always be duplicated in digital tuning based on 100 cents (divisions) per "half step." The human ear—even of a novice—is more sensitive than that. Just a single click of the knob can often go right past the point of an "in tune" perception. Therefore, it seems unlikely that presently available computer-based drills will lead to success in learning to hear and produce well-tuned pitch relations.

Fortunately, computers and digital drills are not essential to accomplish the task. Youngsters reared in acoustic musical environments appear to have little difficulty assimilating natural tuning skills. For the adult who missed that opportunity, the materials contained in "Natural Ear Training" can help. A simple sustained sound source and a willing and curious spirit can lead to the discovery of harmonic reality and musical insight.

Order on line at www.stage3music.com or call 818-704-8657.

More than 15,000 sold!

Lies My Music Teacher Told Me
Second Edition
*Dedicated to all those who studied music just
long enough to be thoroughly confused.*

A number of musical misconceptions are explored and exploded in this humorous and lucid discussion of the relationship between the human perception of music and traditional systems of music education. Drawing on his extensive background in the music world, the author marshals an informal yet rigorous logic to guide the reader through the practical experiences and careful thinking that led him to his conclusion. Updated and refined in the light of reader feedback and more recent thinking, nagging questions such as "Why does formal music training seem not to ensure one's musical success?" are re-addressed. Seekers of musical truth stand to profit from this light-hearted assault on the more nebulous assumptions of the musical community.

Steve Allen - Entertainer, author, TV personality
*We should always be grateful for books—on any subject—that force us to take a
new angle of vision, to interpret familiar things in a fresh way. Dr. Eskelin's
amusing and instructive dissertation does that, and much more.*

Wes Carroll - Massachusetts Institute of Technology
*As a lifelong student of music (and recently-turned-professional performer), I
was delighted to find this new perspective filling in a number of little
holes in my understanding and challenging me to reconsider
some of the ideas I had about music.*

Robert Porter - Undergraduate physics student and violist
*Music has always been presented in such a complicated fashion that I've always
thought it hopeless to truly understand it. Thanks for finally enlightening me.
I think I might give my previous music teachers a visit
and tell them to get this book.*

Dr. Meredith Nisbet - College teacher of music theory and acoustics
*I received an epiphany when I read this book and plan to
immediately incorporate it into my teaching.*

Alan Paul - The Manhattan Transfer
*"Lies" shows in profoundly understandable terms how to
fine-tune one's musical sensibility.*

Tim Smith - Music Reviewer at WUSB Radio, New York
I love this book!!!

Available at major bookstores or call 818-704-8657

Notes

Notes